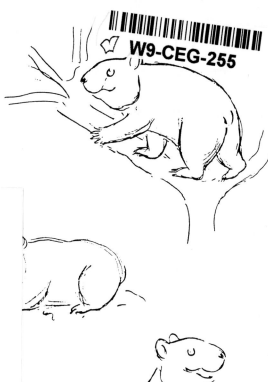

Distributed in the United States by
Smart Apple Media,
1980 Lookout Drive,
North Mankato,
Minnesota 56003

Text copyright © Linda Bygrave
Illustrations copyright © Louise Voce

Consultant: Michael Chinery

ISBN 1-93198-346-1
Library of Congress Control Number 2003102385

Printed in China

I am a Bear

Written By
Linda Bygrave

Illustrated by
Louise Voce

Chrysalis Education

I am a brown bear.
I look like a giant teddy bear,
all soft and cuddly.

But really I'm a big strong animal
and I can be quite fierce.

I cannot see very well.

My eyes are small and weak.

But I have a very good sense of smell.

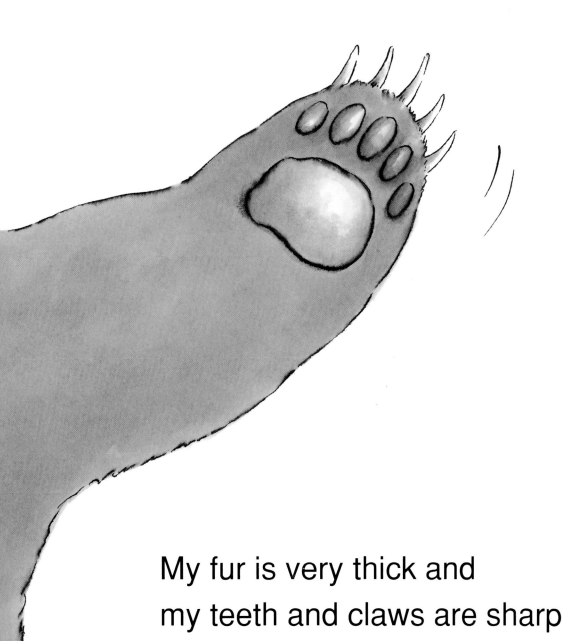

My fur is very thick and
my teeth and claws are sharp.

I have big paws.
Normally I walk on all four feet.

But sometimes I stand up on my hind legs.
Then, I am much taller than your parents!

I like to live in wild places where there are
trees and mountains. I love to scratch
my back against tree trunks.

When I was smaller, I used to climb in the branches.

I am an omnivore. That means
I eat meat as well as plants.
I feed on eggs, nuts, and berries.

I go hunting too, for anything
I can catch!

My favorite food is honey.
I don't feel bee stings through my thick fur.

Sometimes I chase a wolf away from his food. I'm bigger than he is.

In the summertime I go fishing.

I flip the fish out of the river with my big paws, or snap them up in my jaws.

I am a mommy bear.

Over there is a daddy bear.

He is even bigger than me.

We only meet up when it is time
to make some babies.

In the fall, I eat as much as I can
to make myself fat.

This is so that I can sleep all winter
in my nice warm den, without eating.

My babies are born in the winter in my den.
They are called cubs. I have two of them.

My cubs are very small when they are born.
Their eyes are closed, and they have no fur!

My cubs feed on my milk all winter.
They grow very fast. In the spring,
they go outside for the first time.

My cubs play and fight together.
This is good practice for when
they are grown-ups.

I teach them all I know about finding food.
After two years they will leave me
to find homes of their own.

I'm off for a good scratch now.
Good-bye!